DOE/EA-1737

# ENVIRONMENTAL ASSESSMENT

# DOE'S PROPOSED FINANCIAL ASSISTANCE TO PENNSYLVANIA FOR FREY FARM LANDFILL WIND ENERGY PROJECT

# MANOR TOWNSHIP LANCASTER COUNTY, PENNSYLVANIA

## U.S. Department of Energy
## National Energy Technology Laboratory

**February 2010**

# COVER SHEET

**RESPONSIBLE AGENCY:** U.S. Department of Energy (DOE)

**TITLE:** *Environmental Assessment: DOE's Proposed Financial Assistance to Pennsylvania for Frey Farm Landfill Wind Energy Project, Manor Township, Lancaster County, Pennsylvania*

**CONTACT:** For additional copies or more information on this environmental assessment (EA), please contact:

Jane Summerson
EA Document Manager
U.S. Department of Energy
702-292-4290

**Abstract:** PPL Renewable Energy, LLC and the Lancaster County Solid Waste Management Authority propose to construct and operate a 2 turbine wind energy project at the Frey Farm Landfill (FFLF) in Manor Township in Pennsylvania's Lancaster County to provide up to 3.2 megawatts of electricity principally to the adjacent Turkey Hill Dairy. Pennsylvania proposes to provide the project a $1.5 million grant, which would come from a formula grant Pennsylvania received from DOE pursuant to the Department's State Energy Program. This EA analyzes the potential environmental impacts of the proposed construction and operation of the FFLF wind energy project and the alternative of not implementing this project.

**Public Participation:** DOE invited comments on the Draft EA for this project for a period of 12 days beginning with publication of a notice in the Lancaster *Intelligencer Journal* on Wednesday, January 27, 2010. A copy of the Draft EA was made available at the Columbia Public Library, 24 S. 6th Street, Columbia, PA 17512. The public was encouraged to submit written comments regarding the proposed project to DOE by the close of the comment period on February 8, 2010. As of February 10, 2010, DOE had received no comments on the Draft EA.

## ACRONYMS AND ABBREVIATIONS

| | |
|---|---|
| APE | Area of Potential Effect |
| APP | Avian Protection Plan |
| BLM | Bureau of Land Management |
| CFR | Code of Federal Regulations |
| CRGIS | Cultural Resources Geographic Information System |
| DEP | Department of Environmental Protection |
| DOE | Department of Energy |
| EA | environmental assessment |
| FAA | Federal Aviation Administration |
| FFLF | Frey Farm Landfill |
| IBA | Important Bird Area |
| LCSWMA | Lancaster County Solid Waste Management Authority |
| NEPA | National Environmental Policy Act |
| NPDES | National Pollutant Discharge Elimination |
| PDCNR | Pennsylvania Department of Conservation and Natural Resources |
| PEDA | Pennsylvania Energy Development Authority |
| PGC | Pennsylvania Game Commission |
| $PM_{10}$ | particulate matter with an aerodynamic diameter less than or equal to a nominal 10 micrometers |
| $PM_{2.5}$ | particulate matter with an aerodynamic diameter less than or equal to a nominal 2.5 micrometers |
| PNDI | Pennsylvania Natural Diversity Inventory |
| PPL | PPL Renewable Energy, LLC |
| SEP | State Energy Program |
| U.S.C. | United States Code |
| USFWS | U.S. Fish and Wildlife Service |
| WEVCA | Wind Energy Voluntary Cooperative Agreement |

# TABLE OF CONTENTS

## LIST OF TABLES

## APPENDICES

# SUMMARY

PPL Renewable Energy, LLC (PPL), and the Lancaster County Solid Waste Management Authority (LCSWMA) (project proponents) propose to construct and operate a 2 turbine wind energy project at the Frey Farm Landfill (FFLF) in Manor Township in Pennsylvania's Lancaster County to provide up to 3.2 megawatts of electricity, principally to the adjacent Turkey Hill Dairy. After considering a number of alternative turbine configurations and acquiring land to expand the options, the project proponents identified a final proposed layout that has sufficient wind potential and seeks to minimize the potential to injure or kill birds. The turbines would be installed on Turkey Hill Point, which overlooks the Susquehanna River. Each turbine would rise approximately 121 meters (398 feet) and be visible throughout the immediate region.

The Commonwealth of Pennsylvania selected this project for a $1.5 million grant from the Pennsylvania Department of Environmental Protection via the Pennsylvania Energy Development Authority (PEDA). The PEDA grant would come from a Department of Energy (DOE) formula grant pursuant to DOE's State Energy Program (SEP). States can use their SEP funds for a wide variety of activities related to energy efficiency and renewable energy.

In accordance with the National Environmental Policy Act (NEPA), DOE must complete a review of potential environmental impacts of proposals under SEP before making a decision whether to allow states to use the funds for the projects they identify. DOE prepared this environmental assessment (EA), with Pennsylvania's assistance,[1] to analyze the potential environmental impacts of the proposed FFLF Wind Project and an alternative under which the wind project would not be constructed. This EA analyzes the following areas of potential environmental impacts: land use, biological resources, noise, visual quality, transportation, groundwater and surface water resources, soils, air quality and climate change, socioeconomics and environmental justice, energy impacts, cultural resources, and human health and safety.

A primary area of environmental concern for operation of wind turbines is the potential to injure or kill birds and bats. Two species of particular interest in the region of the proposed project site are the bald eagle and the federally listed endangered Indiana bat. Analysis in this EA indicates that the proposed project is not likely to affect the bald eagle's feeding, roosting, or nesting habits. However, there would be a potential for an unavoidable, non-purposeful take of bald eagles due to operation of the proposed wind turbines. Avoidance and minimization measures would reduce possible impacts to bald eagles to the fullest extent practicable, within the constraints of land availability, project economics, and technology. Regarding the Indiana bat, no caves or other places for winter hibernation were identified within a 5-mile radius of the proposed project site. In addition, during construction, 2 acres of trees would be removed, which would eliminate potential Indiana or other bat nesting or roosting sites in the immediate vicinity of the proposed project. In a further effort to avoid and minimize potential impacts to bald eagles and Indiana bats, the area around the wind turbines would be reinvestigated just before construction to verify that bald eagle nests and roost trees are not present.

---

[1] Pennsylvania's role in the preparation of this review was essential. John Hanger, Secretary, Pennsylvania Department of Environmental Protection (DEP), and his staff provided valuable support and information. DOE offers special thanks and recognition to the efforts of Kelly Heffner, Director, Policy Office, DEP, and Catherine Curran Myers, Special Assistant for Pennsylvania Recovery, DEP.

The proposed FFLF Wind Project would generate emissions-free energy that would not degrade air quality. The use of wind power would offset greenhouse gases and other emissions from fossil fuels used to generate electricity, thereby providing an environmental benefit.

The public had at least 18 opportunities over more than 2 years to learn about the project and to provide comments to the LCSWMA and the Manor Township Zoning Board. Between 2007 and 2009, LCSWMA gave 38 public presentations on the FFLF Wind Project to a wide variety of audiences, including industry affiliates, community groups, and private businesses. LCSWMA did not receive any objections to the proposed project at these public presentations. The public was informed of the Draft EA through publication of a notice requesting comment in the *Pennsylvania Bulletin* [40 Pa.B. 562] and the Harrisburg *Patriot-News* on January 23, 2010, and in the Lancaster *Intelligencer Journal* on January 27, 2010. Beginning January 27, 2010, a printed copy of the Draft EA was made available for public review at the Columbia Public Library, 24 S. 6th Street, Columbia, PA 17512, and the Draft EA was available for download from the DOE NEPA Website (http://www.gc.energy.gov/NEPA) and the Pennsylvania Department of Environmental Protection website (http://www.depweb.state.pa.us).

The DOE review of this project has disclosed no significant adverse environmental impacts. Indeed, it strongly suggests that most of the long-term impacts to the environment would be positive.

# 1. INTRODUCTION AND BACKGROUND

PPL Renewable Energy, LLC (PPL), and the Lancaster County Solid Waste Management Authority (LCSWMA) (project proponents) propose to construct a 2 turbine wind energy project at the Frey Farm Landfill (FFLF) in Manor Township in Pennsylvania's Lancaster County to provide electricity to the adjacent Turkey Hill Dairy and, potentially, the regional electricity grid. The current estimated project cost is $8.5 million. The Commonwealth of Pennsylvania selected this project for a $1.5 million grant from the Pennsylvania Department of Environmental Protection via the Pennsylvania Energy Development Authority (PEDA) based on its unique structure (small-scale wind project providing electricity directly to an adjacent commercial end user) that would (1) provide emissions-free energy, (2) create jobs during project construction, and (3) control electricity costs, thereby helping preserve jobs at Turkey Hill Dairy.

A PEDA grant to this project would come from money that Pennsylvania received from the U.S. Department of Energy (DOE) pursuant to DOE's State Energy Program (SEP). The purpose of the SEP is to promote the conservation of energy and reduce dependence on imported oil by helping states develop comprehensive energy programs and by providing them with technical and financial assistance. States can use their SEP funds for a wide variety of activities related to energy efficiency and renewable energy. *See generally* 42 United States Code (U.S.C.) § 6321 *et seq.* and 10 Code of Federal Regulations (CFR) Part 420. In the *American Recovery and Reinvestment Act of 2009* (Public Law 111-5, 123 Statute 115; Recovery Act), Congress appropriated $3.1 billion to DOE for the SEP, and Pennsylvania received $99 million pursuant to a statutory formula for distributing these funds.

Pennsylvania recently informed DOE that it proposes to use $1.5 million of its SEP funds for a grant to the FFLF Wind Project. The potential use of federal SEP funds to assist in the financing of this project constitutes a federal action subject to review under the National Environmental Policy Act (NEPA). Therefore, DOE has prepared this *Environmental Assessment: DOE's Proposed Financial Assistance to Pennsylvania for Frey Farm Landfill Wind Energy Project, Manor Township, Lancaster County, Pennsylvania* (DOE/EA-1737) with Pennsylvania's assistance. This environmental assessment (EA) evaluates the potential environmental consequences of DOE's Proposed Action (allowing Pennsylvania to use $1.5 million of its SEP funds for a grant to this project) and of a No-Action Alternative (not allowing use of SEP funds for this project and assuming, therefore, that the project would not proceed). The EA informs DOE and the public of the potential environmental consequences of these alternatives and mitigating measures that will help reduce these potential consequences.

## 1.1. National Environmental Policy Act and Related Procedures

NEPA, the Council on Environmental Quality NEPA regulations (40 CFR Parts 1500 to 1508), and DOE's NEPA implementing regulations (10 CFR Part 1021) require that DOE consider the potential environmental impacts of a proposed action before making a decision. This requirement applies to decisions about whether to provide different types of financial assistance to states and private entities.

In compliance with these regulations, this EA examines the potential environmental impacts of DOE's Proposed Action and the No-Action Alternative. During the course of preparing this EA, DOE conferred with the project proponents, the United States Fish and Wildlife Service (USFWS), and the Pennsylvania Game Commission (PGC) in order to obtain information on the project and on impacts to avian species, respectively. This EA provides DOE with the information needed to make an informed decision about whether allowing Pennsylvania to use some of its SEP funds for the proposed FFLF Wind Project may result in significant environmental impacts. Based on the EA, DOE either will issue a finding of no significant impact, which could include mitigation measures, or determine that additional study is needed in the form of a more detailed environmental impact statement.

Nothing in this EA affects the project proponents' obligations to comply with the laws of the United States, including the Endangered Species Act, Migratory Bird Treaty Act and the Bald and Golden Eagle Protection Act. Nothing in this EA limits the USFWS's regulatory and permitting authorities under these or any other statutes.

## 1.2. Purpose and Need

### 1.2.1. DOE's Purpose and Need

DOE's purpose and need is to ensure that SEP funds are used for activities that meet Congress's statutory aims to improve energy efficiency, reduce dependence on imported oil, decrease energy consumption, or promote renewable energy. However, it is not DOE's role to dictate to Pennsylvania how to allocate its funds among these objectives or to prescribe the projects it should pursue.

### 1.2.2. Pennsylvania's Purpose and Need

PEDA's purpose and need is to take action to help fulfill its mission to finance clean, advanced energy projects in Pennsylvania, including wind energy projects. Applications are evaluated using criteria including but not limited to technical and financial feasibility of the project, number and quality of jobs created or preserved, and other economic benefits for the Commonwealth of Pennsylvania. Projects must show financial commitment from at least one source other than PEDA and demonstrate a net environmental benefit to Pennsylvania.

## 1.3. Public and Agency Involvement

The public had at least 18 opportunities over more than 2 years to learn about the project and to provide comments to the LCSWMA and, on 2 occasions, to the Manor Township Zoning Board. LCSWMA conducts its business in open public meetings, providing a forum for ongoing reporting and comment on the project ranging from wind and bird studies, to progress on agreements with purchasers, to approving a wildlife assessment agreement with the PGC. The minutes from these meetings are available on the LCSWMA website at http://www.lcswma.org/boardMeetings.asp. These minutes do not identify any public opposition, controversy over resources that would be affected by this project, or suggestions to consider alternatives or mitigation actions not identified in this EA. In addition, no objections were received when the project was presented at the December 9, 2009, meeting of the Manor Township Zoning Hearing Board meeting, which was advertised to and open to the public.

From 2007 through 2009, LCSWMA gave 38 public presentations on the FFLF Wind Project to a wide variety of audiences, including industry affiliates, community groups, and private business. LCSWMA reports that it did not receive any objections to the proposed project at these public presentations. The most recent community meeting was in October 2009.

During this period, the following agencies and organizations were contacted:

- U.S. Fish and Wildlife Service (USFWS)
- Federal Aviation Administration (FAA)
- U.S. Department of Commerce, National Telecommunications and Information Administration
- Pennsylvania Bureau for Historic Preservation
- Pennsylvania Game Commission
- Pennsylvania Department of Conservation and Natural Resources (PDCNR)
- Pennsylvania Fish and Boat Commission
- Manor Township
- Lancaster County Conservation District
- Sprint Nextel

DOE invited comments on the Draft EA for this project for a period of 12 days beginning with publication of a notice in the Lancaster *Intelligencer Journal* on Wednesday, January 27, 2010. A copy of the Draft EA was made available at the Columbia Public Library, 24 S. 6th Street, Columbia, PA 17512, and the Draft EA was available for download from the DOE NEPA Website (http://www.gc.energy.gov/NEPA). The public was encouraged to submit written comments regarding the proposed project to DOE by the close of the comment period on February 8, 2010. As of February 10, 2010, DOE had received no comments on the Draft EA.

In addition, Pennsylvania published a notice requesting comments in the *Pennsylvania Bulletin* [40 Pa.B. 562] and the Harrisburg *Patriot-News* on January 23, 2010, and placed the Draft EA on the Pennsylvania Department of Environmental Protection website (http://www.depweb.state.pa.us). The Department of Environment did not receive comments on the Draft EA.

## 1.4. Considerations Not Carried Forward for Further Analysis

Consistent with NEPA implementing regulations and guidance, DOE focuses the analysis in an EA on topics with the greatest potential for significant environmental impacts. For the reasons discussed below, the proposed wind turbine project is not expected to have any measurable effects on certain resources, and these resources are not analyzed further in Chapter 3.

**Floodplains and Wetlands**

DOE reviewed the USFWS National Wetlands Inventory maps (USFWS, 2009) and Federal Emergency Management Agency (FEMA) floodplain maps (FEMA, 2005) and identified no floodplains, wetlands, or surface water sources such as streams or drainage channels on the proposed project site or that could be affected by the construction and operation of the wind turbines.

**Waste Management**

Solid wastes anticipated to be generated during construction include equipment packaging materials and construction-related material debris. Solid wastes generated during operation of the turbines would be minimal. Solid wastes anticipated to be generated during decommissioning include dismantled equipment and construction-related material debris. Hazardous, regulated non-hazardous, and universal wastes are not anticipated to be generated during construction, operation, or decommissioning. All wastes generated over the life of the proposed project would be managed in accordance with applicable federal, state, and local regulations. Used oil (for example, spent gear box oil, hydraulic fluid, and gear grease) is not considered a waste because it can be reused and/or recycled. Used oil would be generated during project operation, and would be handled, collected, transferred, and reused or recycled in accordance with applicable federal, state, and local regulations.

**Wild and Scenic Rivers**

DOE reviewed the PDCNR Pennsylvania Scenic Rivers Program website (http://www.dcnr.state.pa.us/brc/rivers/scenicrivers/locationmap.aspx) and the National Park Service national rivers inventory website (http://www.nps.gov/ncrc/programs/rtca/nri/states/pa.html). The proposed project site is not located within a waterway, corridor, or drainage area of a stream or river designated as a Pennsylvania Scenic River or a waterway included in the National Wild and Scenic River System. The 2 closest scenic rivers are in Lancaster County (Octoraro Creek and Tucquan Creek, approximately 19 and 8.8 miles from the proposed project site, respectively). The proposed project would not impact federal or state wild and scenic rivers.

**Intentional Destructive Acts**

DOE considers intentional destructive acts (acts of sabotage or terrorism) in its EAs and environmental impact statements (DOE, 2006). Construction and operation of this wind energy project would not involve the transportation, storage, or use of radioactive, explosive, or toxic materials. The project would not offer any particularly attractive targets of opportunity for terrorists or saboteurs to inflict adverse impacts on human life, heath, or safety. In the unlikely event an attack were to occur, its consequences would be similar to those of an accident.

# 2. PROPOSED ACTIONS AND ALTERNATIVES

## 2.1. DOE's Proposed Action

DOE's Proposed Action is to allow Pennsylvania to use its SEP funds for a grant to assist in financing the FFLF Wind Project in order to facilitate Pennsylvania's achievement of the objectives of the SEP.

## 2.2. Pennsylvania's Proposed Project

PEDA selected the FFLF Wind Project for a $1.5 million grant based on its unique structure (small-scale wind project providing electricity directly to an adjacent commercial end user) and its ability to (1) provide emissions-free energy, (2) create jobs during project construction, and (3) reduce Turkey Hill Dairy's electricity costs, thereby helping to preserve jobs at the dairy. A criterion of the PEDA grant program is that the project must be completed by December 31, 2010, and fully operational by February 1, 2011.

The proposed project offers benefits to several parties. LCSWMA would receive a nominal lease payment from PPL for hosting the wind energy project on its property. PPL would fulfill its obligation to provide electricity from alternative energy sources under the Pennsylvania Alternative Energy Portfolio Standards Act. Turkey Hill Dairy would reduce its carbon footprint by purchasing clean power from the project and control energy costs now that rate caps have expired in Pennsylvania. The project also offers the opportunity to teach the public about wind energy through an environmental education center planned for development in the nearby town of Columbia and through public tours of the wind energy facility.

The project would involve construction, operation, and eventual removal of 2 GE wind turbines that would generate approximately 3.2 megawatts of electricity. The height of the turbines' hubs would be approximately 80 meters (262 feet) and the rotor diameter would be approximately 82.5 meters (271 feet), making the total height approximately 121 meters (398 feet). The project would include a new underground electrical distribution line to connect the turbines to existing equipment at the adjacent Turkey Hill Dairy.

Turkey Hill Dairy expects to purchase all the electricity generated by the turbines, which would provide about 25 percent of the dairy's total electrical demand. The distribution line would be connected to the electrical grid so that power also could be sold to Pennsylvania Power and Light for regional distribution.

**Proposed Site**
The proposed FFLF Wind Energy project would be located atop Turkey Hill Point overlooking the Susquehanna River, southwest of the city of Lancaster, south of Washington Borough, and southwest of the town of Creswell in Lancaster County's Manor Township (Figure 1, Appendix A). The site is on the perimeter of the active landfill, which is situated between River Road and the Susquehanna River at Lake Clarke (Figure 2, Appendix A). The proposed locations for Wind Turbines A and B are shown on Figure 3 in Appendix A; these locations are closest to

tower locations T-1 and T-5 marked on Figure 4 in Appendix A. Entrance to the FFLF is from River Road. The approximate center point of the FFLF is at Latitude/Longitude 39° 57' 22.42"/76° 27' 15.10".

**Construction**
Construction would include installation of the 2 turbines, underground distribution line, necessary access roads and road improvements, crane pads, foundation systems, and fencing around the proposed site. It would be performed in accordance with an approved erosion and sedimentation control plan, National Pollutant Discharge Elimination System (NPDES) permit, and in compliance with all other applicable requirements. Wind turbine installation, including site preparation, erection, and final commissioning, generator installation, underground distribution line installation, and overall systems tie-in and start-up is planned to be completed within about 4 months of project start.

Construction also would entail clearing approximately 2 acres of trees. The trees planned for removal are young white pines (*Pinus strobus*) (approximately 1 acre) along the landfill's former perimeter fence and some relatively young deciduous trees (approximately 1 acre) along the northwestern property line.

There would be a transformer at the base of each wind turbine to boost the voltage to 12,000 volts (12 kilovolts). An underground distribution line would be routed east in a straight path through a new duct bank from the wind turbines for approximately 2,440 feet, where it would be connected to an existing underground duct bank (Option A, Figure 3, Appendix A). The wire would then be pulled through the existing duct bank to connect with Turkey Hill Dairy's existing switchbox. A duct bank protects electrical or other cables from damage by soil, moisture, puncture, and other sources of potential damage. There is no need for a conventional transmission line, a substation, or extensive wiring.

The new section of concrete-reinforced duct bank would be installed in an excavated trench approximately 4.5 feet deep and 2.5 feet wide. The proposed route would cross previously disturbed areas consisting of maintained land within the landfill property and would parallel an access road adjacent to agricultural land. Efforts would be made to minimize disturbance to the agricultural lands. Alternative options would require disturbance of a larger area and additional costs associated with extending the length of the duct bank.

During construction, the contractor would provide necessary facilities consistent with similarly sized construction projects, including construction trailer, temporary chemical toilets, and solid-waste collection containers. All solid and liquid wastes would be removed from the site in accordance with applicable regulations and permit conditions.

Due to the unique characteristics of the site (see Section 2.3.3), there were no other reasonable areas for placing the project on LCSWMA property. The project proponents evaluated 5 potential turbine locations within the project area to determine the best locations for minimizing harm to birds. The size of the project is the minimum needed to maintain economic viability for the project proponents.

**Operation**

PPL and LCSWMA would operate and maintain the wind energy project according to standard industry procedures and applicable requirements. Routine maintenance of the turbines would be necessary to maximize performance and identify potential problems or maintenance issues. Each turbine would be remotely monitored daily to ensure operations are proceeding efficiently. Any problems would be reported to operations and maintenance personnel, who would perform both routine maintenance and most major repairs. Most servicing would be performed up-tower, without using a crane to remove the turbine from the tower. In addition, all roads, pads, and trenched areas would be regularly inspected and maintained to minimize erosion.

**Decommissioning**

The turbine and other infrastructure are expected to have a useful life of at least 20 years. Pursuant to the Zoning Hearing Board of Manor Township variance approval, the project proponents must provide a plan for the removal of wind turbine A when it becomes functionally obsolete or is no longer in use. The project proponents also would decommission turbine B consistent with the variance requirements.

The trend in the wind energy industry has been to "repower" older wind energy projects by upgrading equipment with more efficient turbines, thereby extending the project's useful life beyond 20 years. When the project is terminated, the turbine and other infrastructure would be decommissioned, and all facilities would be removed to a depth of approximately 3 feet below grade. Underground facilities could be removed, or safely secured and left in place. Salvageable items (including fluids) would be sold, reused, or recycled as appropriate; unsalvageable material would be disposed of at authorized sites. The soil surface would be restored as close as possible to its original condition. Reclamation procedures would be based on site-specific requirements commonly employed at the time the area is to be reclaimed and could include regrading, adding topsoil, and replanting of all disturbed areas.

## 2.3. Alternatives

### 2.3.1. DOE Alternatives

Pennsylvania's SEP funds are from a formula grant – the amount is determined pursuant to a formula established in DOE grant procedures at 10 CFR 420.11. Allocation of funds among the states is based on population and other factors. Recipients of these formula grants have broad discretion in how they use their funds. Accordingly, DOE's alternatives to its Proposed Action relating to Pennsylvania's use of its SEP funds are limited to (1) any alternatives that Pennsylvania is still considering regarding this project and (2) prohibiting Pennsylvania from providing a grant to this project. The second alternative is equivalent to the No-Action Alternative described in Section 2.3.2. Pennsylvania has informed DOE that it is not considering any "project-specific" alternatives for the FFLF Wind Project; therefore, DOE's alternatives are limited to the No-Action Alternative. Additionally, there are no unresolved conflicts concerning alternative uses of available resources associated with the project site that would suggest the need for other alternatives.

### 2.3.2. No-Action Alternative

Under the No-Action Alternative, DOE would not allow Pennsylvania to use its SEP funds for this project. DOE assumes for purposes of this EA that the project would not proceed without SEP funding. This assumption could be incorrect, but it allows for a comparison between the potential impacts of the project as proposed and the impacts of not proceeding with the project. Without the proposed project, FFLF operations would continue as otherwise planned but without the proposed wind turbines, and the Turkey Hill Dairy would continue purchasing electricity as it does now. Pennsylvania's ability to use its SEP funds for energy efficiency and renewable energy activities would be impaired, as would its ability to create jobs and invest in the nation's infrastructure in furtherance of the goals of the Recovery Act.

### 2.3.3. Alternatives Considered by the Project Proponents

During the more than 2 years of the project's development, PPL and LCSWMA considered several alternative locations for the wind turbines (Figure 4, Appendix A). The project proponents eliminated all but the 2 proposed locations due to various siting considerations (topography, site elevation, prevailing wind direction), avian considerations, location (proximity to electrical interconnection, proximity to the meteorological tower location, accessibility), physical siting constraints (landfill footprint, property boundaries, adjacent trail), and turbine spacing.

The wind energy project was originally conceived of as having 4 turbines with approximately 6 megawatts of capacity (tower locations T-1, T-2, T-3, and T-4). Based on the results of a spring bird migration survey, project biologists estimated that potential impacts to wildlife could be reduced by moving the turbines inland from Turkey Hill Point and by reducing their number to 2. At that time, a fifth possible tower location (T-5) was identified on a neighboring parcel to the north of FFLF, away from the riverine forested corridor and back from the steep riverine slope. LCSWMA purchased the parcel in September 2009 and added T-5 to the fall raptor/eagle migration survey.

The project proponents selected the locations of proposed wind turbine A (near T-1) and wind turbine B (near T-5) based on the siting considerations and constraints described below.

**Siting Considerations**
The project proponents performed various studies to determine potential impacts to avian species (see Section 3.2.2). These studies found, for example, that observations of eagles within the potential rotor-swept zone varied by location, with 68 at T-2, 65 at T-4, 53 at T-1, 43 at T-3, and 31 at T-5. Tower location T-2 in spring and fall had the greatest number of observations recorded for all species of special concern. Overall, tower location T-4 had the most occurrences of all birds within its rotor-swept zone. When considering all raptors/eagles, T-1 and T-5 had the fewest occurrences of species within a possible rotor-sweep zone. Turkey vultures and black vultures were recorded within the zones of all 5 potential tower locations.

Proposed wind turbine A would be a short distance from the location analyzed for tower location T-1, and proposed wind turbine B would be 232 feet southwest of tower location T-5.

The project proponents changed the locations to minimize potential impacts to avian species; maintain necessary siting requirements with respect to increasing the setbacks from the river and riverine forested habitat; and satisfy property line, access road, and utility setbacks. The results of the 2009 fall migration survey for tower locations T-1 and T-5 correlate to proposed wind turbines A and B, respectively. Based on the wind characteristics of the site, physical siting constraints, and the results of the raptor/eagle migration surveys, the project proponents determined that wind turbine locations A and B are the most favorable with respect to minimizing potential impacts to wildlife while maintaining the economic viability of the project.

The proposed turbine locations are on Turkey Hill Point, which extends out into the Susquehanna River at Lake Clarke and forms a steep bluff adjacent to the river. This unique landform is responsible for producing higher wind speeds at the proposed project site than in surrounding areas because the wind must accelerate up and over the steep bluff. Only the northern and western edges of the FFLF are suitable for a wind energy project due to the need to have uninterrupted exposure to the west-northwesterly prevailing wind direction. In addition to favorable exposure to the prevailing wind, the northern and western edges of the FFLF are the highest elevations at the site, which results in higher sustained wind speeds. Based on these features, a 22-month wind resource assessment was performed at the site using information collected from a meteorological tower on the northwestern edge of the landfill. According to the project proponents, the wind resource assessment provided the basis for energy production estimates that demonstrated the viability of the project.

The project proponents also considered in their siting proposal that the turbines should be near the electrical interconnection point at Turkey Hill Dairy and in accessible locations that would minimize new road construction. The proposed locations are within 1 mile of the interconnection point to deliver energy to Turkey Hill Dairy, which would minimize environmental disturbances and reduce construction costs. The turbine locations also are adjacent to the active landfill, which is a compatible land use for the wind energy project because accessibility would be available for construction and maintenance and overall environmental impacts associated with new access road construction would be reduced.

Wind turbine orientation and spacing also were important criteria in the siting process. The proposed wind turbines at FFLF would be situated roughly perpendicular to the prevailing wind direction to maximize energy generation. Additionally, the proposed turbine locations are separated by the minimal spacing needed to prevent wake interference between the turbines.

Physical siting constraints at the landfill also were considered and include the active landfill footprint; property boundaries; existing utilities; and the Turkey Hill Trail. Siting wind turbines on an active landfill is not allowed because foundation stability requirements would not be satisfied. Therefore, possible turbine locations were limited to the western and northern periphery of the FFLF. Existing utilities (such as the PPL high voltage electrical transmission line and the Sprint-Nextel cellular tower) limited the movement of the proposed turbine locations farther east. Moving the turbines farther west was limited by the steep bluff and by proximity to the Turkey Hill Trail.

One other underground distribution line alignment (Option B, Figure 3, Appendix A) was evaluated. This option would have entailed "piggybacking" the distribution line on the existing utility poles that extend from near the proposed wind turbines to the existing landfill gas-to-energy facility and then continuing the line in an underground duct bank to Turkey Hill Dairy. This option would have required a significant lengthening of the distribution line, adding substantial cost to the project. The Manor Township Zoning Ordinance requires all transmission or distribution lines from renewable energy projects to be underground; therefore, an aboveground option would have required a variance. The aboveground option also would pose a greater risk of electrocution to birds and other wildlife species. Due to these considerations, the project proponents concluded that Option B was not a viable option for the distribution line.

### 2.3.4. Alternatives Considered by Pennsylvania in the PEDA Grant Process

In 2009, the Pennsylvania Department of Environmental Protection received 389 PEDA applications seeking more than $400 million. Eleven projects were competitively selected to receive $10 million in Recovery Act funding. Thirteen additional projects were competitively selected to receive $10.7 million in state funding.

## 2.4. Required Agency Permits and Approval Types

Prior to construction, all required federal, state, and local permits and approvals would be obtained. Table 2-1 lists the required permits and approvals.

**Table 2-1.** Federal, State, and Local Permits and Approvals

| Agency | Permit Approval/Type |
|---|---|
| **Federal** | |
| Federal Aviation Administration | Aeronautical Determination (Received 12/22/2009) |
| National Telecommunications and Information Administration | Radio Frequency Transmission Approval (Received 01/05/2010) |
| **State** | |
| Pennsylvania Department of Environmental Protection | National Pollutant Discharge Elimination System |
| Pennsylvania Historic and Museum Commission | Compliance with the Pennsylvania History Code Compliance with the National Historic Preservation Act |
| Pennsylvania Game Commission | Compliance with the Wind Energy Voluntary Cooperation Agreement |
| **Local** | |
| Manor Township Zoning Board | Variance Approval (Received 01/06/2010) |
| Lancaster County Conservation District | Erosion and Sediment Control Plan Approval |

In addition, the project proponents are coordinating with the USFWS to comply with the Bald and Golden Eagle Protection Act and Migratory Bird Treaty Act in an effort to avoid and minimize impacts to avian species as a result of the project.

## 2.5. Project Proponents' Commitments

PPL and LCSWMA have committed to the following measures and procedures to minimize or avoid potential environmental impacts of the proposed project.

**Concentration Areas and Landscape Features Known to Attract Birds**
Birds are known to use the wooded habitat along the Susquehanna River. To minimize potential impacts to avian species, the proposed turbine locations were moved as far back from the Susquehanna River corridor as practicable. LCSWMA purchased an additional 16 acres of land adjacent to the FFLF to facilitate the relocation of the proposed turbines to the north of the landfill and to accommodate a desired setback from the Susquehanna River.

**Reduce Number of Turbines**
The project proponents reduced their project from 4 wind turbines to 2. The reduction eliminated the turbines with the most potential to affect avian species (i.e., those located farther west toward the river).

**Turbine Configuration**
The proposed wind turbines would be configured to avoid potential avian mortality, where feasible. The turbines would be spaced as close together as possible following recommended USFWS interim guidance (USFWS, 2003). The proposed turbine locations were moved away from the river corridor to the extent possible. The turbine configuration balances potential impacts to wildlife with wind patterns, siting requirements, and topographic conditions.

**Bird, Bat, and Raptor Avoidance and Minimization Measures**
All American kestrel and Eastern Bluebird nest boxes in the vicinity of the proposed wind turbine locations have been removed. This will reduce the attractiveness of the project area to these species.

The project proponents have entered into a voluntary cooperative agreement with PGC (Wind Energy Voluntary Cooperation Agreement) to work collaboratively to ensure that the proposed wind energy project is developed in an environmentally conscientious manner and with best regard to the conservation of wildlife resources. The agreement includes post-construction monitoring surveys for 2 years to assess mortality of avian species and bats. PGC and USFWS would be notified if any threatened or endangered species were found during post-construction mortality surveys. PGC and USFWS would consult (as part of the adaptive management approach) regarding the need for any additional project proponents-committed measures based on the findings of the post-construction surveys.

Construction of the wind turbines and associated facilities would commence before the beginning of the 2010/2011 bald eagle nesting season (which can begin in late November and continue through August) to avoid construction disturbance to any new nests that might occur in the vicinity of the proposed project. (Based on surveys conducted in December 2009 and January 2010, the nearest nest is more than 1 mile away across the Susquehanna River [ARM, 2010a]). If construction did not commence before the 2010/2011 nesting season, a new aerial nesting survey would be performed and provided to the USFWS and PGC for review.

An Avian Protection Plan (APP) would be prepared and submitted to the USFWS for approval before commencement of construction activities. The USFWS Avian Protection Plan Guidelines (2005) would be used to develop the APP. These guidelines were primarily developed to address avian electrocution and collision impacts associated with transmission lines. However, these guidelines have been used, with USFWS approval, for wind power projects (Iberdrola Renewables, 2008). An APP supports practices and processes intended to minimize impacts to birds, with a goal of implementing a series of best practices to avoid or reduce risks to birds. Because every project is different, the USFWS guidance is used as a "tool box" from which a utility can select and tailor components applicable to specific needs. The following components would be implemented as part of the APP for the project:

- Make a reasonable effort to construct and alter wind turbines to reduce the instance of avian mortality (this component has been completed via turbine siting and configuration).
- Obtain and comply with all legally required permits.
- Monitor incidents of avian mortality (this component is already part of the project).
- Report to USFWS any takes of bald eagles that occur as a result of the wind turbines during the operational life of the project.
- Train personnel on avian issues such as reporting avian mortalities and disposal of carcasses.
- Develop an avian reporting system.
- Identify avian experts that can be called upon to resolve avian issues, which could include state or federal resource agencies, universities, or conservation groups.
- Identify adaptive management protocols.
- Adopt decommissioning conservation measures.

**Habitat Restoration**
The design plans would include measures to minimize potential impacts to wildlife following construction and during the operation phase of the project. Grass beneath the wind turbines would be regularly cut to reduce the value of the habitat for wildlife and decrease habitat attractiveness for wildlife. Existing nest boxes in the vicinity of the proposed wind turbines have been removed.

**Turbine Design**
Guy wires would not be used to support the wind turbines. Guy wires can be a challenge for birds and bats to locate, which makes them difficult to maneuver around and can lead to injury or death. Also, lattice towers, which have become roosting sites for birds at other wind projects, would not be used to support the wind turbines.

**Aviation Lighting**
Aviation lighting would comply with FAA requirements to minimize impacts to birds and bats. White strobe lights would be used in the minimum number, intensity and number of flashes per minute allowed by the FAA. Solid red or pulsating red warning lights would be avoided. The project has received final approval from the FAA (see Appendix C).

**Health, Safety, and Noise**
The construction contractor and facility operator would prepare a Health and Safety Plan in accordance with Occupational Safety and Health Administration requirements before

commencing work. Facilities would be secured by fencing and include signs warning of high voltage. All construction activities would occur during normal working hours to avoid noise and other disturbances to surrounding residences. Construction of the proposed wind energy project would comply with all applicable federal, state, and local requirements.

**Erosion Control**

The Lancaster County Conservation District is responsible for administering the erosion control program in Lancaster County (Pennsylvania Department of Environmental Protection Chapter 102 erosion control regulations). The project proponents would prepare and implement an Erosion and Sediment Pollution Control Plan, which would also address and NPDES requirements (for projects grading more than 1 acre) and would submit the plan to the Lancaster County Conservation District for an Erosion and Sediment Pollution Control Plan adequacy determination.

**Invasive Species Control**

Voluntary cleaning of equipment and vehicles during construction and operation, using clean fill and mulch, and avoiding planting of invasive species would be employed at the project site. The conservation measures would be included as notes on the construction drawings to help conserve sensitive plant habitats.

**Recycling**

Used oil would be generated during project operation, and would be handled, collected, transferred, and reused or recycled in accordance with applicable federal, state, and local regulations.

# 3. AFFECTED ENVIRONMENT AND ENVIRONMENTAL IMPACTS

## 3.1. No-Action Alternative

If the FFLF Wind Project is not implemented, the 25 percent of Turkey Hill Dairy's electrical power that could be provided by the project would continue to be purchased from Pennsylvania Power and Light. That utility generated about 60 percent of its total electricity with fossil fuels in 2008 (PPL, 2009). The remaining 40 percent of generation came from sources that do not directly emit carbon dioxide (renewables and nuclear). Thus, carbon dioxide emissions from electricity generation to serve the dairy would be higher under the No-Action alternative and Turkey Hill Dairy would not meet its objective to reduce its carbon footprint.

Baseline conditions would continue pursuant to current FFLF plans. Specifically, soil storage would continue in the project area. Under the No-Action alternative, there would be no impacts to the area's visual resources and no noise impacts as a result of the project. Potential impacts to bird species, including the bald eagle, from operation of the wind turbines would not occur. The small number of jobs created by construction and operation of the wind turbines would not be realized and the local area would forego the economic benefit associated with these new jobs. The road improvements required for the project would not be made and resulting impacts would not occur.

## 3.2. Pennsylvania's Proposed Project

### 3.2.1. Land Use

The land use pattern beyond the boundaries of the FFLF and surrounding the proposed wind energy project site is primarily rural residential/agricultural with patches of wooded areas consisting of stream corridors, fence rows, and wood lots. The landfill itself is in the excavation zoning district as indicated on the Zoning Map of Manor Township, and the adjacent Turkey Hill Dairy facility has an industrial zoning designation. The proposed project area is in the rural zoning district. There is an active railroad corridor under the ownership of Pennsylvania Lines, LLC (also known as Norfolk Southern Railroad), immediately adjacent to the river to the west of the project site. The railroad property is in the conservation zoning district. Wind energy conversion systems are allowed in both the rural and conservation zoning districts as uses accessory to "public uses and public utilities structures," as defined in the Township's zoning ordinance. The most contiguous patch of forestland occurs on the steep slopes of the Susquehanna River corridor and is situated between the active railroad corridor and the active landfill. The forested corridor along the river is, overall, approximately 400 feet wide, with a slope of approximately 75 percent.

The proposed project area is situated along the northern and northwestern perimeters of the active landfill and the edge of the forested corridor along the Susquehanna River. The proposed project area is on 16 acres of former agricultural land purchased by FFLF in September 2009. Most of the 16 acres would remain an open area, with a portion occupied by the 2 turbines and related equipment and several acres used for a soil stockpile area for the landfill. Existing vegetation in the proposed project area consists primarily of active hay fields, maintained grass areas, and herbaceous vegetation on soil stockpiles.

Manor Township's Zoning Ordinance does not impose height restrictions on wind energy conversion systems provided that the height of the systems is not greater than the shortest distance measured along a horizontal plane from the unit to any property boundary. A zoning variance was approved by the Zoning Hearing Board of Manor Township on January 6, 2010, granting the LCSWMA relief from the property line setback requirement for wind turbine A (see Appendix C).

The project area is in the vicinity of the Turkey Hill Trail, which is maintained by the Lancaster County Conservancy. The trail is in a wooded area down-slope of the proposed turbine locations. The forested habitat surrounding the trail might serve as a buffer, especially during the growing season, to minimize effects on visual quality. The closer of the 2 turbines would be approximately 450 feet from the trail. The trail is beyond the length of a turbine at its fully extended height. The trail receives the most use during summer and fall. As explained in Section 3.2.3 of this EA, noise emitted from the operation of the wind turbines is not expected to affect hikers using the trail.

The proposed wind energy project is in the immediate vicinity of the Susquehanna River at Lake Clarke. Lake Clarke is an 11.5-square-mile lake bordered by York County to the west and Lancaster County to the east, and is used for recreational activities such as boating, sailing, canoeing, swimming, waterfowl hunting, fishing, and bird watching. Lake Clarke is in a designated Pennsylvania Fish and Boat Commission water trail section that extends 52 miles from Harrisburg, Pennsylvania, to the Maryland border. The proposed wind project would be visible from the lake, but is not expected to affect recreational activities at the lake. The section of river nearest the project area, including Lake Clark, is an Audubon Pennsylvania-designated Important Bird Area (IBA), Conejohela Flats IBA #56 (see Section 3.2.2 for more discussion on this IBA).

## 3.2.2.   Biological Resources

Birds and bats can be injured or killed if they fly into operating wind turbines. In addition, birds, bats, and vegetation could be disturbed by construction and decommissioning activities associated with the proposed project. The USFWS, PGC, and PDCNR are responsible for protecting various plant and animal species and associated habitat in the proposed project area. A primary emphasis of these agencies is to ensure that appropriate actions are taken to reduce or mitigate potential harm to protected species and habitat.

To identify potentially affected species and habitat, the project proponents first used the Pennsylvania Natural Diversity Inventory (PNDI), which is found on the PDCNR Pennsylvania

Natural Heritage Program website (http://www.naturalheritage.state.pa.us/). This was followed by direct contact with the USFWS, PDCNR, and PGC. PNDI search results did not indicate any reason to coordinate with the Pennsylvania Fish and Boat Commission, and no coordination with the Commission was undertaken. Appendix B includes the results of the initial online inquiry and follow-up communication.

### 3.2.2.1. Bald Eagles and Other Migratory Birds

The PNDI review reported three species under PGC jurisdiction within the proposed project area – the great egret (*Casmerodius albus*), a Pennsylvania endangered species; the prothonotary warbler (*Protonotaria citrea*), a species of special concern; and an unidentified sensitive species listed as Pennsylvania threatened. Following review of the PNDI report and other project information, PGC reduced to 2 the number of species requiring further coordination – the great egret (*Ardea alba*[2]) and bald eagle (*Haliaeetus leucocephalus*), a Pennsylvania threatened species (see Appendix B, PGC letter dated November 30, 2009). The bald eagle is no longer a federally listed species pursuant to the Endangered Species Act, but it is protected by the Migratory Bird Treaty Act[3] and the Bald and Golden Eagle Protection Act. Thus, project proponents also coordinated with USFWS regarding project planning and establishing mitigation measures.

The lower Susquehanna River is a known avian migratory pathway. Conejohela Flats IBA #56 provides breeding and foraging habitat for birds and is an important resting and feeding area during migration. The bird species of concern in the IBA vicinity include the bald eagle, great egret, and osprey (*Pandion haliaetus*), Pennsylvania threatened; peregrine falcon (*Falco peregrines*), Pennsylvania endangered; and northern harrier (*Circus cyaneus*), Pennsylvania at-risk. These species are protected by state wildlife protection regulations and the Migratory Bird Treaty Act.

**Wind Turbines and Bird Mortality**
Avian mortality rates from collisions with wind turbines vary by location, species, and turbine technology (GAO, 2005). Erickson et al. (2001) estimated the national average collision-related mortality for all birds at wind farms to be approximately 2.19 birds per turbine per year. Excluding California, the average mortality rate drops to 1.83 birds per turbine per year. The large number of older turbines operating in California is one reason for a disproportionately high number of bird deaths associated with wind projects in that state (GAO, 2005). The Government Accountability Office reviewed 30 studies of avian mortality and found that overall bird fatalities range from 0 to 7.28 birds per turbine per year (GAO, 2005).

For the proposed FFLF Wind Project, the primary concern is potential impacts to bald eagles and other raptors (birds of prey). Erickson et al. (2001) estimated the national average collision-related mortality for raptors at wind farms to be approximately 0.033 raptors per turbine per year, or 0.006 raptor fatalities per turbine per year when excluding California. The Bureau of Land Management (BLM) reviewed 18 wind farms in 11 states – including a western Pennsylvania

---

[2] The great egret has 2 scientific names: *Casmerodius albus* and *Ardea alba*.
[3] The Migratory Bird Treaty Act prohibits any "take," including to pursue, shoot, shoot at, poison, wound, kill, capture, collect, molest, or disturb.

wind farm, Somerset Wind Energy Center – and found that the number of raptor collisions ranged from 0 fatalities per turbine per year for eight of the wind farms to 0.48 fatalities per turbine per year. The Somerset wind farm recorded no raptor or bird fatalities during monitoring. In the Appalachia region of the United States, raptor fatalities ranged from 0 to 0.07 raptor fatalities per turbine per year (GAO, 2005).

BLM compared bird abundance and post construction mortality studies at several existing wind farms across the United States and found that there was little correlation between species that are present in an area and those that are killed in collisions with wind turbines (BLM, 2005). More recently, de Lucas (2008) also found that that there was no clear relationship between collision fatality of raptors at wind farms and raptor abundance.

Researchers have observed raptor behavior that suggests some species are able to avoid wind turbines. BLM (2005) concluded that not all species are prone to collisions at wind farms, probably through a combination of their typical flight patterns, their abilities to perceive the turbines, and their abilities to avoid the turbines. Young et al. (2003) recorded several instances in which birds were observed avoiding turbines. Raptors were observed altering their flight paths to avoid turbines, and in one case, a golden eagle turned around and flew back the way it had come when it approached a turbine. Several different species of raptors and large birds were observed positioning themselves around turbines while maintaining the same flight course. Golden eagles were observed climbing above the level of the spinning blades to pass over turbines.

BLM (2005) notes that no bald eagles have been reported to be killed at any wind power farm in the western states. Erickson et al. (2001) also compared bird mortality rates at various wind developments and found a similar pattern of no bald eagles being killed. Generally, raptors are able to avoid wind turbines (Young et al., 2003) and the number of raptors killed at any facility is small (NWCC, 2002). Depending on the species involved and its population size, the number of fatalities might or might not result in population-level effects to the affected raptors. No studies have shown population-level effects in raptor populations associated with wind energy projects (BLM, 2005).

**FFLF Avian Studies**
Due to the presence of bird species of concern and the proximity of a migratory pathway, the project proponents performed 4 avian studies in 2009 and 2010. Each of the studies was provided to USFWS and PGC:

- 2009 Raptor and Eagle Migration Survey - March 2009 (ARM, 2009)
- Bald Eagle and Osprey Nest Survey - December 21, 2009 (ARM, 2010a)
- 2009 Fall Migration Survey - August 15 to December 15, 2009 (ARM, 2010b)
- Bald Eagle Winter Roost Survey - January 2010 (ARM, 2010c)

The migration surveys followed PGC's *Protocols to Monitor Bird Populations at Industrial Wind Turbine Sites* (PGC, 2007). The aerial nest survey was reviewed with PGC and USFWS at an agency coordination meeting December 14, 2009. The plan of study for the winter roost survey was provided to PGC and USFWS before the study was performed.

The aerial nest survey and winter roost survey identified no bald eagle nests within 1 mile of the project area and no bald eagle winter roost areas in the project area. The nearest bald eagle nest is more than 1 mile west of the proposed project area, across the Susquehanna River.

A total of 174 hours of observation were recorded during the spring survey and 647.2 hours were recorded during the fall survey. Tower location T-5 was not part of the project during the spring survey, but was accounted for in the fall survey. The objectives of the surveys were to:

- Determine the species, number, and frequency of migratory raptors and eagles within the proposed wind turbine area.
- Identify the potential for impacts to raptors and eagles.
- Assess the potential risk to raptors and eagles at each turbine location.
- Assist in siting and design to avoid and minimize potential impacts to raptors and eagles.
- Serve as a technical document for state and federal agencies during the review process.

Parameters recorded during observations included flight direction, height of flight, flight altitude, relationship to the proposed wind turbines, type of flight (direct, indirect, soaring hunting, or perching), weather data, and observation duration. Observers also recorded sector-to-rotor zone (circular zone outline by the tips of the turning rotor blade) identified as Sector A, the west or north side of the proposed turbine area; Sector B, along the summit within a 200-meter swath, where turbines would likely be situated; and Sector C, the east (or south) slope of the zone, but not within 100 meters of the mountain top or spine (see Figure 5, Appendix A).

A total of 12 and 14 species of raptors/eagles were observed during spring and fall surveys, respectively. Turkey vultures and black vultures represent the largest number of recorded species during both surveys. Bald eagles were the fifth most recorded raptor during the spring survey (2 percent of the total species observed) and third most recorded during the fall survey (8.3 percent of the total species observed). A daily passage rate of 1.1 eagles per hour was observed during the spring survey, while 6.9 eagles per hour were observed during the fall survey. Overall, tower locations T-1 and T-5 had the fewest observed raptor species within a turbine zone. Tower locationT-5 had the fewest occurrences of raptors/eagles observed and the fewest occurrences of raptor species of concern (eagles, osprey, peregrine falcon, and northern harrier) within a possible rotor-swept zone of the turbine. Tower locations T-2 and T-4 had the most occurrences of raptors/eagles within a possible rotor-swept zone based on both migration surveys. Tower location T-2 in spring and fall had the greatest number of observations recorded for the raptor species of special concern identified above.

PGC (2008) noted that the bald eagle observations in fall might be related to raptor risk level. According to the fall migration survey, the FFLF is a high risk site for raptors because 559 bald eagles and 2 unidentified eagles were observed in the vicinity of the proposed wind turbine locations. The "observations" record the number of times an eagle or raptor enters the sectors being observed. It does not reflect the total number of eagles or raptors observed because one individual could be counted several times.

**Potential Impacts during Construction**

Construction noise and activities are known to disturb the nesting and foraging behaviors of bald eagles and other bird species. To avoid nesting disturbance of bald eagles, all turbine and related facility construction would begin outside the nesting season (late November through August; *National Bald Eagle Management Guidelines* [USFWS, 2007]). Winter 2009-2010 aerial nesting survey results indicated that the nearest bald eagle nest is more than 1 mile away from proposed construction activities (ARM, 2010). Nest building for the 2010 breeding season was well underway at the time of the winter nesting survey; therefore, it is highly unlikely that any new nests would occur in the vicinity of the wind turbine project during this season. Construction is planned to begin in late summer 2010. In the event construction is not completed by December 2010, bald eagles looking to build nests for the 2011 breeding season would likely avoid the construction area due to the ongoing disturbance.

Nesting bald eagles generally forage within 2 to 3 miles of their nest (BLM, 2005). Construction activities could disturb a portion of this foraging range for the bald eagle nest more than 1 mile to the west. However these effects would be temporary and isolated to the area of disturbance directly surrounding the proposed project area. Decommissioning activities would be similar to construction and would likely require that conservation measures similar to the proposed construction measures be implemented. Because decommissioning is at least 20 years away, and conditions in the area could change, decommissioning conservation measures would be included in the APP developed and provided to the USFWS for approval, and measures would allow for adaptive management if necessary. At a minimum, the decommissioning conservation measures in the APP would include decommissioning timing constraints so that this activity occurs outside the bald eagle and raptor nesting season, or, if that timing is not feasible, performing an aerial nesting survey before decommissioning and establishing appropriate buffers (determined in coordination with USFWS and PGC) if a nest was encountered during the aerial nest survey.

**Potential Impacts during Turbine Operation**

Based on 2 wind turbines, less than one raptor fatality per year at FFLF is expected assuming an average mortality rate of 0.07 raptors per year per turbine (the high end of the range identified in studies summarized above) and 2.8 raptor fatalities would be expected over 20 years of operation). Because this risk estimate considers all raptors, potential bald eagle fatalities are expected to be even less.

Operation of the wind turbines could disturb bald eagle or other raptor foraging in the vicinity of the landfill. However, FFLF accepts mostly inorganic materials such as ash residue and construction debris, so there is minimal odor and minimal scavenging by birds (ARM, 2010b). No raptors were documented in the landfill during ARM raptor migration surveys (ARM, 2010b). Operation noise from the wind turbines would not be expected to affect bald eagle nesting or foraging because the noise levels would be low. At a distance of approximately 350 meters (~1,150 feet), sound from wind turbines is in the range of 35 to 45 A-weighted decibels, similar to the background noise found in a typical home (AWEA, 2009). To put this into perspective, decibel levels of 60, 50, 40, and 30 are equivalent to conversational speech at 1 meter, an average home, a quiet library, and a quiet bedroom at night, respectively.

**Agency Coordination and Planned Mitigation**

The project proponents would implement avoidance and minimization measures to reduce possible impacts to bald eagles, to the extent practicable, within the constraints of land availability, project economics, and technology. If construction of the wind turbine project did not commence before the start of the bald eagle nesting season in 2010 (late November), an additional nesting survey would be completed and provided to USFWS and PGC for review and approval. In an effort to further minimize potential impacts to bald eagles and other raptors, the area encompassing a radius of 660 feet around wind turbines A and B (full rotor extent) would be investigated just before construction of the wind turbines to verify that bald eagle or other raptor nests and roost trees are absent and to ensure conservation of species. If such nest or roost trees were found, the project proponents would notify USFWS and PGC to determine what avoidance measures to implement. In addition, the project proponents would prepare an Avian Protection Plan and submit it to USFWS for approval; the plan would include the elements listed in Section 2.5.

The project proponents initiated formal coordination efforts with USFWS and PGC via letter on October 6, 2009, and October 28, 2009, respectively. These coordination efforts have continued and all FFLF avian studies have been provided to both USFWS and PGC. Appendix B includes copies of written correspondence related to this coordination effort.

PGC requested that additional surveys in accordance with the protocols described in the Wind Energy Voluntary Cooperative Agreement (WEVCA) be conducted. PPL and PGC executed the WEVCA in December 2009. The WEVCA provides measures to avoid and minimize impacts to the bald eagles, great egrets, and other wildlife species. Appendix B includes a copy of the signed WEVCA. As part of the WEVCA, 2 years of post-construction monitoring would be implemented to monitor impacts to birds and bats and to assess impacts to other species of concern.

The project proponents have participated in several calls with USFWS to develop and agree on additional avoidance and minimization measures. DOE has separately participated in calls with USFWS, and participated in conference calls with several parties, including USFWS, to discuss this issue. DOE communications with USFWS include a call between the 2 agencies on February 1, 2010, and a conference call with USFWS, PGC, and the project proponents on February 4, 2010. As a result of these efforts, the project proponents have added the following conservation measures: develop an Avian Protection Plan (described in Section 2.5), construct the turbines outside the bald eagle nesting season (which would avoid noise and other construction-related disturbance of nesting bald eagles, raptors, and other migratory bird species), and perform ongoing post-construction mortality surveys. These conservation measures would augment the measures previously committed to by the project proponents (entering into the WEVCA, adaptive management in cooperation with the USFWS, and 2 years of post-construction avian mortality studies).

The potential for an unavoidable, non-purposeful take of the bald eagle exists at the project site, due to the installation of the proposed wind turbines. However, based on the findings of the avian surveys and a review of pertinent literature as discussed above, the project would not be likely to adversely affect the bald eagle's feeding, roosting, or nesting habits. Additionally, based on recent communications with USFWS and planned implementation of additional conservation measures, DOE has determined that the proposed wind project, which would include construction and operation of the wind turbines in compliance with all USFWS permitting and other requirements, would have no significant impact on the bald eagle.

### 3.2.2.2. Indiana Bat

The PNDI review did not identify state or federal endangered or threatened bat species in the project area. However, during subsequent communications, the USFWS stated that, while the federally listed endangered Indiana bat (*Myotis sodalist*) is not known to occur within the proposed project boundaries, there could be potential habitat in the area. Both USFWS and PGC recommended that the project proponents search the proposed project area for potential bat hibernacula (places providing a constant temperature and protection during winter hibernation) (see Appendix B, USFWS letter, November 13, 2009, and PGC letter, November 30, 2009).

The project proponents searched the PNDI, Natural Heritage Inventory of Lancaster County, Pennsylvania (update 2008), and Natural Heritage Inventory of York County, Pennsylvania (2004 amended) (http://www.naturalheritage.state.pa.us/CNAI_Download.aspx) to determine if caves potentially providing habitat for bat hibernacula were known within a 5-mile radius of the project area. They identified no caves supporting bats of concern within 5 miles of the proposed project area. In addition, ARM biologists performing other field investigations on the FFLF site report that they observed no caves.

The Indiana bat uses trees for roosting and nesting. The proposed project site contains wooded areas that could provide roosting or nesting habitat. Approximately 2 acres of trees would be removed before March 31, 2010, in the vicinity of wind turbines A and B to minimize potential impacts to nesting bats. The trees planned for removal are relatively young white pines (approximately 1 acre) along the landfill's former perimeter fence and some relatively young deciduous trees (approximately 1 acre) along the northwestern property line. Representative tree species along the perimeter of the project area include northern hackberry (*Celtis occidentalis*), black cherry (*Prunus serotina*), black locust (*Robinia pseudoacacia*), pawpaw (*Asimina triloba*), and red maple (*Acer rubrum*). Oak species (*Quercus* sp.) and hickory species (*Carya* sp.) are present farther down slope, closer to the river. Many of the trees are overgrown with mile-a-minute (*Polygonum perfoliatum*) and river bank grape (*Vitis riparia*), making them less suitable for nesting. Indiana bats are not known to use white pine trees for roosting or nursing.

Based on these investigations and mitigation commitments and DOE's review of documents in the record, DOE has determined that the proposed project would have no effect on the Indiana bat. Therefore, DOE does not need to enter into informal or formal consultation with the USFWS under Section 7 of the Endangered Species Act.

### 3.2.2.3. Plant Species

Vegetation in the proposed project area consists of maintained grass, vegetated stockpiles, and former agricultural lands. The lands that would be primarily affected by the wind energy project have been disturbed by landfill activities and agricultural use. In the PNDI review, 2 plant species of concern were identified under the jurisdiction of PDCNR – scarlet ammannia (*Ammannia coccinea*), Pennsylvania endangered, and the tooth-cup (*Rotala ramosiori*), a state species of special concern. The PNDI review indicated that no further consultation with PDCNR is necessary as long as conservation measures are implemented. Conservation measures include voluntary cleaning of equipment/vehicles, use of clean fill and mulch, and avoiding planting invasive species. The project proponents would include these conservation measures as notes on the construction drawings to ensure they are implemented.

### 3.2.3. Noise

The proposed project area is on the western and northern boundaries of an active landfill. The existing noise environment is characterized by heavy landfill equipment operating 6 days a week and by other nearby activities such as a railroad; a gas-to-energy facility with 2 engines operating 24 hours a day, 7 days a week; and Turkey Hill Dairy's manufacturing and processing facilities. The nearest noise-sensitive receptors (occupied dwellings) to the proposed wind energy project are on River Road approximately 2,250 feet east of tower location T-5. This residential area is east of the Turkey Hill Dairy.

Noise would be emitted from the project site by construction equipment during the approximately 4-month construction period. However, due to the distance to the closest noise-sensitive receptor and the noise-generating activities at the adjacent active landfill, wind energy project construction noise would not be expected to increase the overall ambient noise emissions from the site.

Modern wind turbines are generally quiet in operation and the sound is very low compared to that of road traffic, trains, aircraft, and construction activities. Modern wind turbines have been designed to drastically reduce the noise of mechanical components, so the most audible noise is the sound of the wind interacting with the rotor blades. At a distance of approximately 350 meters (~1,150 feet), sound from wind turbines is in the range of 35 to 45 A-weighted decibels, similar to the background noise found in a typical home (AWEA, 2009).

The noise from the proposed wind project would not be expected to affect noise-sensitive receptors, given the distance to the nearest receptor (approximately 2,250 feet) and the other noise-generating activities between the project site and the receptor. The sound emitted from the project would be attenuated by the distance to the receptor. In addition, all of the additional noise sources would act to "drown out" the minimal sound generated from the wind energy facility.

While hikers on the Turkey Hill Trail could experience temporary noise impacts from the project site during the estimated 4-month construction period, the trail and project site are adjacent to an active landfill where construction equipment operates and generates construction-type noise 6 days a week, year round. Additionally, there are a number of other permanent noise sources in the area, such as the railroad. The noise emitted from the operation of the wind turbines would not be expected to affect hikers using the trail.

### 3.2.4. Visual Quality

The existing view of the project area is primarily rural/residential and agricultural, with adjacent government facilities and a dairy operation. There are some vertical features, including a Sprint cellular tower in the immediate vicinity of the project area. Other area features do not have a strong vertical component and are not immediately visible from many viewpoints. The nearest viewers are employees at the FFLF and adjacent dairy. Three occupied dwellings were identified within approximately 2,250 feet of the project location. There are scattered residences farther east and southeast of the project location. Due to their location atop Turkey Hill, and depending on the vantage point, the turbines would be visible from a distance of 10 miles from certain directions on a clear day. This includes viewpoints along the Susquehanna River and at Lake Clarke. The ability to see discrete features at a distance of 5 to 10 miles is limited by weather conditions, visual acuity, structures and clusters of trees, and other factors.

While it is not possible to quantify the visual impact of a wind energy project due to the subjective nature of aesthetics, visual impacts are sometimes a concern with such projects. Concerns about the visual impacts of wind energy projects generally revolve around aesthetic impacts and shadow flicker impacts associated with the rotating turbines. To address potential concerns about the aesthetic impacts of the proposed project, LCSWMA held a public meeting on October 14, 2009, for Manor Township residents and presented rendered images of what the project would look like from various vantage points within the surrounding communities, including views from the western bank of the Susquehanna River in York County. Appendix D includes copies of these renderings and a map of the viewing points. Following the public meeting, there was no correspondence from any members of the township objecting to the project on the basis of visual impacts. Furthermore, there was no public opposition to the project at the Manor Township Zoning Hearing Board meeting in December 2009, at which time a zoning variance from setback requirements was requested to construct the project.

In addition to preparing the renderings of the project, the project developers commissioned a study to determine if any nearby occupied dwellings would be adversely affected by shadow flicker from the project. Appendix D includes the shadow flicker analysis, which concluded that while 5 occupied dwellings within a 1-mile radius of the turbines could experience shadow flicker effects for approximately 2 hours per year, the proposed siting of the turbines conforms to industry standards and no substantial adverse shadow flicker impacts would result from developing the wind energy project at the proposed location.

Overall, there are no anticipated visual impacts that would significantly affect nearby residents and users of the project area and surrounding areas as a result of the development of this project.

### 3.2.5. Transportation

During the project construction phase, a temporary increase in vehicular traffic on the local roads surrounding the project site would be anticipated. This modest traffic increase would occur for a period of approximately 4 months. No long-term or permanent impacts to the local transportation systems would occur as a result of this project.

Large pieces of equipment such as turbine towers, rotor blades, and nacelles that would be designated oversized loads would temporarily slow traffic on Route 30 and some local roads, such as River Road, as they were moved into the project area. Additionally, minor road improvements or adjustments might be needed to deliver the extended-length components to the project site. Any necessary road closures would be temporary and would only apply to the roads immediately surrounding the project site. Any damage to the local road network as a result of delivering project equipment would be fully mitigated and repaired by the project developer.

### 3.2.6. Groundwater and Surface Water Resources

In compliance with the Clean Water Act and Pennsylvania's Clean Stream Law, there were no streams identified in the project area based on observations made by biologists and geologists visiting the project area. An erosion swale was identified to the northwest of tower location T-3, and another erosion swale was identified northeast of location T-5. Both erosion swales carry surface water runoff during heavy precipitation events. There are no private well-water supplies on or near the project site.

The Susquehanna River is approximately 500 feet from the wind turbine locations. The Susquehanna River is classified as Warm Water Fishes and Migratory Fishes at this location, according to the Pennsylvania Code Title 25, Chapter 93, Water Quality Standards. The closest stream to the wind turbines with a high-quality designation is Wisslers Run, which is approximately 3,000 feet to the north of the proposed project area. Wisslers Run is designated as High Quality-Cold Water Fishes and Migratory Fishes, according to the Pennsylvania Code Title 25, Chapter 93, Water Quality Standards. Wind turbine B would be closest to the Wisslers Run watershed. However, due to distance, overland flow from the proposed project area would not reach Wisslers Run. A Lancaster County Conservation District approved Erosion and Sediment Pollution Control Plan would be implemented before, during, and following construction.

The proposed distribution line (Option A, Figure 3, Appendix A) would consist of a concrete reinforced duct bank installed in an excavated trench with approximate dimensions of 4.5 feet deep and 2.5 feet wide. Approximately 1,710 feet of this buried duct bank would be within the Susquehanna River watershed, which includes Mann's Run subwatershed. The Susquehanna River and Mann's Run at this location do not have a high-quality or exceptional-value protected water-use designation, according to Title 25 of the Pennsylvania Code, Chapter 93, Water Quality Standards. The remaining approximately 730 feet is within the Wisslers Run watershed, a High-Quality Cold Water Fishes and Migratory Fishes watershed, according to Title 25 of the Pennsylvania Code, Chapter 93, Water Quality Standards. However, the installation of the duct bank would occur within an area of the Wisslers Run watershed that drains directly to an existing, NPDES-permitted and maintained detention basin on Turkey Hill Dairy property (Figure 3, Appendix A). No runoff or discharges from the proposed excavation area would directly enter Wisslers Run. An NPDES permit would be acquired prior to any earthwork related to the installation of the duct bank. All trench excavation and any other related ground-disturbing work would be in conformance with an approved Erosion and Sedimentation Pollution Control Plan specific to this project.

### 3.2.7.   Soils

The following soils are located in the vicinity of the 5 possible tower locations based on review of the Soil Survey of Lancaster County, Pennsylvania (USDA, 1985):

- Glenelg silt loam, 3 to 8 percent slopes
- Glenelg silt loam, 8 to 15 percent slopes
- Manor silt loam, 8 to 15 percent slopes
- Manor Stony Silt Loam, 8 to 25 percent slopes
- Manor Stony Silt Loam, 25 to 60 percent slopes

Glenelg silt loam is listed as prime farmland soils and Glenelg silt loam and Manor silt loam are listed as soils of statewide importance for Lancaster County, Pennsylvania. The locations of T-2, T-3 and T-4 are within the Glenelg silt loam soil type, but the soils have been disturbed from landfill operations. Wind turbine A (immediate vicinity of T-1) and wind turbine B (immediate vicinity of T-5) would be in a parcel that was previously farmed but no longer in agricultural use because a portion of the parcel is being used for landfill soil stockpiling activities. The proposed location of wind turbine A is in the vicinity of Glenelg silt loam. Therefore, soils in the vicinity of the proposed wind turbines have already been disturbed.

Site preparation and project construction would result in soil disturbance. As part of project construction, approximately 2 acres of wooded area would be lost and the total area of disturbance would be less than 10 acres. Ground-disturbing activity requires compliance with the Pennsylvania Department of Environmental Protection Chapter 102 erosion control regulations, including the preparation and implementation of an Erosion and Sediment Pollution Control Plan. The Lancaster County Conservation District, through a delegation agreement with the Pennsylvania Department of Environmental Protection, is responsible for administering the Erosion Control Program in Lancaster County. In addition to the required Erosion and Sediment Pollution Control Plan, earthmoving projects that disturb more than 1 acre might require an NPDES Permit. Pursuant to the Chapter 102/NPDES delegation, the Erosion and Sediment Pollution Control Department staff reviews plans, issues NPDES Permits, and performs site inspections. After an Erosion and Sediment Pollution Control Plan is reviewed and determined to be adequate, a determination of adequacy letter is issued. If an NPDES permit is needed, the Lancaster County Conservation District would issue the NPDES permit concurrently with or shortly after the Erosion and Sediment Pollution Control Plan adequacy determination.

An approved Erosion and Sediment Pollution Control Plan, in compliance with NPDES, would be implemented before, during, and following construction activities. On-site quality assurance inspectors would ensure that the erosion and sediment pollution control measures are implemented and properly installed and maintained.

### 3.2.8.   Air Quality and Climate Change

The affected air environment can be characterized in terms of concentrations of the criteria pollutants carbon monoxide, sulfur dioxide, particulate matter, nitrogen dioxide, ozone and lead. The U.S. Environmental Protection Agency has established National Ambient Air Quality

Standards for these pollutants. There are 2 standards for particulate matter, one for particulates with an aerodynamic diameter less than or equal to a nominal 10 micrometers ($PM_{10}$) and one for particulates with an aerodynamic diameter less than or equal to a nominal 2.5 micrometers ($PM_{2.5}$). According to the Environmental Protection Agency Mid-Atlantic Air Protection website (http://www.epa.gov/reg3artd/airquality/airquality.htm), Lancaster County, Pennsylvania, is in non-attainment for $PM_{2.5}$ and ozone (listed as "marginal" for both 1-hour and 8-hour ozone). Lancaster County is in attainment for carbon monoxide, sulfur dioxide, $PM_{10}$, nitrogen dioxide, and lead.

The proposed wind energy project at the FFLF would be an emissions-free energy generation project that would not degrade air quality. Aside from temporary dust generated during construction and decommissioning, which would be minimized to the extent practicable (for example, by keeping gravel on roads and watering dry roads), this project would not result in any adverse impacts to air quality. The project would not require any air permits.

It is assumed that if the wind energy project was not built, the electricity used by Turkey Hill Dairy would continue to be supplied primarily by fossil-fuel sources. Pennsylvania Power and Light generated about 60 percent of its total electricity in the United States with fossil fuels in 2008 (Pennsylvania Power and Light Company, 2009). The proposed FFLF Wind Project would generate approximately 7,500,000 kilowatt-hours per year, which would offset greenhouse gases (approximately 4,300 tons per year of carbon dioxide equivalents) and other emissions from the use of fossil fuels to generate electricity (ICF, 2010).

## 3.2.9. Socioeconomics and Environmental Justice

The proposed wind energy project would be in Lancaster County's Manor Township. The county's population in 2006 was approximately 494,000 and the population of Manor Township in 2000 was approximately 16,500 (U.S. Census Bureau, 2000). The economy of Lancaster County is a diverse combination of manufacturing, agricultural, transportation, and service industries. Major local employers in Manor Township include the Turkey Hill Dairy. Construction of the proposed project would create temporary jobs, and operation and maintenance of the proposed wind turbines would be expected to create new permanent jobs. The temporary construction jobs would last approximately 4 months and would not cause population increases in the area. The additional permanent jobs would be expected to be filled by residents of the local area and would not cause a population increase. The area's public and community services, such as schools, health care, social services, and fire protection, would not be affected by the proposed project. No residences, businesses, or industries would be negatively affected or relocated as a result of the proposed wind energy project. The additional permanent jobs would provide a benefit to the local economy.

Executive Order 12898 (February 11, 1994) directs federal agencies to identify and address "disproportionately high and adverse human health or environmental effects of its programs, policies, and activities on minority populations and low-income populations." The racial makeup of Manor Township in 2000 was 95.6 percent White, 1.4 percent African American, 0.1 percent American Indian, 1.3 percent Asian, 0.8 percent from other races, and 0.9 percent from 2 or more races. People identifying themselves as Hispanic or Latino of any race made up 2.3 percent of the population. The median income for a household in Manor Township in 2000 was $47,806, compared to $41,994 for the United States. About 2.4 percent of families and 3.8 percent of individuals in Manor Township were below the poverty line (U.S. Census Bureau, 2000).

The proposed wind project would be adjacent to an active landfill and at least 2,250 feet from the closest residential area, which is on River Road. No potential high and adverse impacts to human health or environmental effects have been identified in this EA. There would be no disproportionately high and adverse human health or environmental effects on minority populations and low-income populations.

### 3.2.10. Energy Impacts

The proposed wind energy project would have a nameplate capacity of 3.2 megawatts and generate approximately 7,500,000 kilowatt-hours per year, or enough electricity to supply up to 700 homes each year. The wind energy generated from the proposed project would meet approximately 25 percent of Turkey Hill Dairy's annual electricity needs. If the project did not move forward, it is assumed that the electricity used by Turkey Hill Dairy would continue to be supplied primarily by fossil-fuel sources, which are finite. The proposed renewable energy project would produce significant amounts of clean electricity for the 20-year design life of the project. No adverse energy impacts would result from the project.

### 3.2.11. Cultural Resources

Neither the Pennsylvania Inventory of Historic Places nor the National Register of Historic Places lists any state or federal historic resource within the proposed project area. No known National Register-eligible sites were identified in the Area of Potential Effect (APE) of the proposed wind turbines or the proposed electrical distribution line. Also, there are no known sites within the proposed project area on the National Registry of Natural Landmarks according to the National Park Service webpage (http://www.nature.nps.gov/nnl/), which shows the localities of national natural landmarks.

A portion of the National Register-eligible Enola Branch Rail Line, Atglen & Susquehanna Branch, is located along the Susquehanna River in the vicinity of the APE. However, direct and indirect effects to the resource would not be anticipated. The project proponents initiated consultation with the Pennsylvania Historical and Museum Commission on January 21, 2010, to obtain concurrence on these conclusions (see Appendix B).

The Pennsylvania Historical and Museum Commission Cultural Resources Geographic Information System (CRGIS) indicates the presence of potential prehistoric archaeological sites within the proposed project area. Two potential prehistoric archaeology sites were mapped in the project area as part of a separate soil stockpile project for the FFLF. One of the sites is in the vicinity of tower location T-2 in an area disturbed by the landfill, and CRGIS indicates the site was not recommended as eligible for listing on the National Register of Historic Places. The other site (36LA939) was identified in the vicinity of the 2 proposed wind turbine locations. A Phase I archaeological survey was performed by a qualified archaeologist in October 2009 in the area of the proposed wind turbines. The Phase I findings appear consistent with the mapped location of the known site, thus confirming the presence of the site. However, the artifact recovery was low and no temporally diagnostic artifacts were recovered. The Pennsylvania Historical and Museum Commission concurred with the survey findings that further investigation of the site would not yield data significant to the prehistory of the region (see Appendix B). The site was not considered eligible for listing in the National Register of Historic Places and further archaeological investigation was not recommended by the Pennsylvania Historical and Museum Commission. If any prehistoric archaeological site were encountered during construction, the contractor would stop work in that area, while the project proponents consult with the Pennsylvania Historical and Museum Commission on the need for appropriate evaluative studies, determinations of National Register eligibility, and potential mitigation measures, as required by the National Historic Preservation Act.

## 3.2.12. Human Health and Safety

Workers can be injured or killed during construction, operation, and decommissioning of wind turbines through industrial accidents such as falls, fires, and dropping or collapsing equipment. Such accidents are uncommon in the wind industry and are avoidable through implementation of proper safety practices and equipment maintenance. All contractors, subcontractors and their personnel would be required to comply with all federal and state worker safety requirements. The construction contractor and facility operator would prepare a Health and Safety Plan pursuant to Occupational Safety and Health Administration requirements before commencing work, and by following this plan, greatly reduce the potential for worker injuries and fatalities.

If members of the pubic were to attempt to climb towers or open electrical panels, they could be injured or killed. Public access to the proposed project area would be restricted by a 6-foot-high security fence. Safety signage would be posted around all towers, transformers and other high-voltage facilities, and along roads in conformance with applicable federal and state regulations.

Two major accident scenarios associated with turbines are the collapse of a turbine and breakage of one or more turbine blades. The potential for the proposed turbines to fall over or collapse causing damage, injury, or death would be remote. Foundations are designed to prevent turbines from falling over, but 5 of the 13,000 GE turbines operating globally have collapsed since 2002 (Bogdan, 2009). For example, in March and October 2009, 1.5-megawatt GE turbines collapsed in Altona and Fenner, New York, respectively. Similarly, blades have broken off wind turbines, but such events are rare. In either case, the impacts would depend on the direction of the falling turbine or dislodged blade and who or what was in the path. In most directions, the impact would be on LCSWMA property with little potential for damage. Turbine A would be approximately 450 feet from the Turkey Hill Trail, which is maintained by the Lancaster County Conservancy. If that turbine fell in the direction of the river, there is a potential to topple trees on the steep slope and to impact the trail. Another potential source of accidents is ice shedding and ice throw. GE has established recommendations to mitigate this risk (http://www.gepower.com/prod_serv/products/tech_docs/en/wind_turbines.htm).

The proposed project area is not in the vicinity of a local or regional airport or a military air base. All structures more than 61 meters (200 feet) tall must have aircraft warning lights in accordance with requirements specified by the FAA. Both turbines would have such lighting. The FAA has issued a Determination of No Hazard to Air Navigation for the proposed wind project (see Appendix C).

Lubricants are used in wind turbines, including gearbox oil, hydraulic fluid, and gear grease that require periodic replacement. These lubricants would be managed in accordance with federal and state regulations. Any accidents involving potential spills of gear box oil, hydraulic fluid, and gear grease would be contained and cleaned up to minimize environmental impacts and slip, trip, and fall hazards. In addition, PPL and LCSWMA would require that fueling and lubrication of equipment and motor vehicles be performed in a manner to protect against spills and evaporation and that unused lubricants and oils be disposed of in approved manners and locations.

# 4. CUMULATIVE IMPACTS

Cumulative impacts are potential environmental impacts that result "from the incremental impact of the action when added to other past, present, or reasonably foreseeable future actions regardless of what agency (Federal or non-Federal) or person undertakes such actions. Cumulative impacts can result from individually minor but collectively significant actions taking place over a period of time" (40 CFR 1508.7).

## 4.1. Reasonably Foreseeable Projects

DOE reviewed information on past, present, and reasonably foreseeable future projects and actions that could result in impacts over the same period and in the same general location as the proposed wind energy project. Based on this review, DOE identified the following three projects as appropriate for inclusion in the cumulative impacts analysis:

- FFLF opened in 1989 and currently is expected to operate through 2020. FFLF consists of 96 acres and includes 5 disposal cells. A Resource Recovery Facility, Household Hazardous Waste Facility, and Waste Management Transfer Complex also are located at the landfill. The Resource Recovery Facility is a waste-to-energy facility that processes up to 1,200 tons of solid waste per day. Under planned operations, a portion of the cleared area closest to the proposed wind turbines would be used for soil storage.

- LCSWMA is exploring a plan to vertically expand landfill capacity in the area of the proposed project. Current plans include employing a mechanically stabilized earthen berm around the perimeter of the existing FFLF to add an additional 10 million cubic yards of capacity (approximately doubling the current capacity) without a substantial change in footprint. The earthen berm could be up to 60 feet high in places. Construction is not expected until 2017 or 2018 under current planning scenarios (LCSWMA, undated).

- The Turkey Hill Dairy is to the northwest of the FFLF. It produces milk, ice cream, ice teas, and fruit drinks.

## 4.2. Summary of Cumulative Impacts

**Biological Resources**

PGC recently reported that approximately 175 active bald eagle nesting pairs produced approximately 242 fledglings in 2009 in 48 counties of Pennsylvania. This represents an increase from approximately 156 nests and approximately 171 fledglings in 2008 and approximately 132 nests and 151 fledglings in 2007. Pennsylvania's bald eagle population is increasing at a rate of 15 percent per year (PGC, 2009). An approximate 90-percent success rate for active nests has been reported, which represents 1.6 young per successful nest from 2007 to 2009. Pennsylvania bald eagles have produced at least 1,400 eaglets over the past 20 years (Gross, 2009). The population trends recorded by Audubon between 1967 and 2006 show an average annual increase of bald eagle sightings of 14.4 percent for Pennsylvania, which represents the second highest of any state (Audubon, 2007).

Based on these growth trends, it is likely that the bald eagle will continue to expand its existing population throughout the Lower Susquehanna River basin due to abundant habitat availability and food supply. Like any tall structure (such as communications towers and high-voltage transmission towers) constructed within the known habitat of the bald eagle, the proposed wind turbines present the potential for an unavoidable, non-purposeful take of bald eagles. However, project proponents would implement avoidance and minimization measures to reduce possible impacts to bald eagles to the extent practicable within the constraints of land availability, project economics, and technology.

**Noise**
Noise from the proposed project would be localized (see Section 3.2.3) and add to the noise levels in the immediate project vicinity. Other noises from the project vicinity are intermittent, such as the noise from passing vehicles on area roads, noise that would be generated during the planned vertical landfill expansion, and noise resulting from FFLF operations. While the turbines would add to background noise levels, these levels, even when added to noise sources from the activities listed in Section 4.1 and other local activities, would not be likely to cumulatively impact area residents or change the semi-rural nature of the area.

**Visual**
The wind turbines would be the dominant vertical component in the landscape due to their total height of 121.25 meters (398 feet). The vertical expansion of the landfill would also have visual impacts, but they would be localized and potentially screened by vegetation. Cumulative impacts to visual resources could affect users of the Turkey Hill Trail. Trail users would experience a change in visual quality due to the impacts of the wind turbines and landfill expansion.

**Greenhouse Gas**
While the scientific understanding of climate change continues to evolve, the Intergovernmental Panel on Climate Change Fourth Assessment Report stated that warming of Earth's climate is unequivocal, and that warming is very likely attributable to increases in atmospheric greenhouse gases caused by human activities (anthropogenic) (IPCC, 2007). The Fourth Assessment Report indicates that changes in many physical and biological systems, such as increases in global temperatures, more frequent heat waves, rising sea levels, coastal flooding, loss of wildlife habitat, spread of infectious disease, and other potential environmental impacts are linked to changes in the climate system, and that some changes could be irreversible (IPCC, 2007).

The release of anthropogenic greenhouse gases and their potential contribution to global warming are inherently cumulative phenomena. It is assumed that this wind energy project would displace fossil-fuel electricity currently used at Turkey Hill Dairy, resulting in a net decrease in emissions of approximately 4,300 tons of carbon dioxide equivalents for each year of operation. The proposed project would neither reduce the concentration of greenhouse gases in the atmosphere nor reduce the annual rate of greenhouse-gas emissions. Rather, it would minimally decrease the rate at which greenhouse-gas emissions are increasing every year and contribute to ongoing global efforts to reduce greenhouse gases and slow climate change.

# 5. REFERENCES

ARM (ARM Group, Inc.). 2009. 2009 Spring Raptor and Eagle Migration Survey - Proposed Wind Energy Project at Frey Farm Landfill. Prepared for Lancaster County Solid Waste Management Authority and PPL Development Company, LLC.

ARM (ARM Group, Inc.). 2010a. Bald Eagle Osprey and Nest Survey - Proposed Wind Energy Project at Frey Farm Landfill. Prepared for Lancaster County Solid Waste Management Authority and PPL Development Company, LLC.

ARM (ARM Group, Inc.). 2010b. 2009 Fall Raptor and Eagle Migration Survey - Proposed Wind Energy Project at Frey Farm Landfill. Prepared for Lancaster County Solid Waste Management Authority and PPL Development Company, LLC.

ARM (ARM Group, Inc.). 2010c. Bald Eagle Winter Roost Survey - Proposed Wind Energy Project at Frey Farm Landfill. Prepared for Lancaster County Solid Waste Management Authority and PPL Development Company, LLC.

Audubon. 2007. Audubon Christmas Bird Count Data 1967-2006. Published June 26. Available at http://audubon.org/news/pressroom/Bald_eagle/eagle_chart.pdf.

AWEA (American Wind Energy Association). 2009. Wind Energy Fact Sheet -- Utility Scale Wind Energy and Sound
Available: http://www.awea.org/pubs/factsheets/Utility_Scale_Wind_Energy_Sound.pdf

BLM (Bureau of Land Management). 2005. *Final Programmatic Environmental Impact Statement on Wind Energy Development on BLM-Administered Lands in the Western United States*. Prepared by Argonne National Laboratory for BLM, Washington, D.C. Available at http://windeis.anl.gov/documents/fpeis/index.cfm Accessed January 29, 2010.

Bogdan, J. 2009. *Responsibility for Toppled Turbine Cloudy. The Observer-Dispatcher*. December 28. Available at http://www.uticaod.com/news/x1437795639/Responsibility-for-toppled-turbine-cloudy Accessed February 07, 2010

de Lucas, Manuela, et al. 2008. Collision fatality of raptors in wind farms does not depend on raptor abundance. Journal of Applied Ecology 45:6, 1695-1703. Online publication date: 9-Oct-2008. Abstract available at http://www.ingentaconnect.com/content/bsc/jappl/2008/00000045/00000006/art00018 Accessed January 29, 2010.

DOE (U.S. Department of Energy). 2006. Memorandum. Office of NEPA Policy and Compliance. *Need to Consider Intentional Destruction Acts in NEPA Documents*. December 1, 2006.

Edison Electric Institute's Avian Power Line Interaction Committee (APLIC) and U.S Fish and Wildlife Service (USFWS). 2005. Avian Protection Plan Guidelines, April 2005.

Erickson, W.P., Johnson, G.D., Strickland, M.D., Young, D. P. 2001. Avian collisions with wind turbines: a summary of existing studies and comparisons to other sources of avian collision mortality in the United States, Report to the National Wind Coordinating Committee (Cheyenne, Wyoming: NWCC). Available at http://www.west-inc.com/reports/avian_collisions.pdf Accessed January 29, 2010.

FEMA (Federal Emergency Management Agency). 2005. https://hazards.fema.gov/wps/portal/mapviewer Accessed January 20, 2010. Effective date: April 19, 2005.

GAO (U.S. Government Accountability Office). 2005. Wind Power Impacts on Wildlife and Government Responsibilities for Regulating Development and Protecting Wildlife. Available at www.gao.gov/new.items/d05906.pdf

Gross, Douglas. 2009. Pennsylvania Game Commission Wildlife Biologist, Endangered Bird Specialist and PA Bird Coordinator.

Iberdrola Renewables. 2008. Avian and Bat Protection Plan. Available at http://www.iberdrolarenewables.us/pdf/Signed_ABPP_10-28-08.pdf Accessed February 3, 2010.

ICF (ICF International). 2010. Carbon Dioxide Emissions Calculation.

IPCC (International Panel on Climate Change). 2007. Fourth Assessment Report, Climate Change 2007: Synthesis Report

LCSWMA (Lancaster County Solid Waste Management Authority). Undated. *Future Landfill Expansion Issue.*

NWCC (National Wind Coordinating Committee). 2002. Permitting of Wind Energy Facilities: A Handbook, Siting Subcommittee, c/o RESOLVE, Washington, D.C., March. Available at http://www.nationalwind.org/assets/publications/permitting2002.pdf Accessed February 1, 2010.

PGC (Pennsylvania Game Commission). 2007. *Protocols to Monitor Bird Populations at Industrial Wind Turbine Sites* http://www.dcnr.state.pa.us/info/wind/documents/final_draft-bird_pre_and_post_feb_23_2007.pdf
..

Pennsylvania Power and Light Company. 2009. *PPL Sustainability Report 2009 – Climate Change.* Available: http://www.pplweb.com/corporate+responsibility+report/2008/environmental+-+climate+change.htm

Census Bureau. 2000. Available: http://www.census.gov/main/www/cen2000.html Accessed January 20, 2010.

USDA (U.S. Department of Agriculture). 1985. Soil Survey of Lancaster County Pennsylvania. Available: http://soildatamart.nrcs.usda.gov/manuscripts/PA071/0/Lancaster.pdf USDS-Soil Conservation Service.

USFWS (U.S. Fish and Wildlife Service). 2003. *Interim Guidelines on Avoiding and Minimizing Impacts from Wind Turbines,* May 13, 2003.

USFWS. 2007. National Bald Eagle Management Guidelines, May 2007.

USFWS. 2009. National Wetlands Inventory. http://www.fws.gov/wetlands/Data/Mapper.html. Accessed January 20, 2010. Published September 25, 2009.

Young, D.P., et al. 2003. Comparison of Avian Responses to UV-Light-Reflective Paint on Wind Turbines, NREL/SR-500-32840, National Renewable Energy Laboratory, Golden, Colo., Jan. Available at http://www.west-inc.com/reports/fcr_nrel.pdf Access January 29, 2010.

# 6. AGENCIES AND PERSONS CONSULTED

U.S. Fish and Wildlife Service
Pennsylvania Field Office
315 South Allen Street, Suite 322
State College, PA 16801-4850

National Telecommunications and Information Administration
Herbert C. Hoover Building (HCHB)
U.S. Department of Commerce / NTIA
1401 Constitution Avenue, N.W.
Washington, D.C. 20230

Federal Aviation Administration
Air Traffic Airspace Branch, ASW-520
2601 Meacham Blvd.
Fort Worth, TX 76137-0520

Pennsylvania Historical and Museum Commission
Bureau for Historic Preservation
Commonwealth Keystone Building, 20d Floor
400 North Street
Harrisburg, PA 17120-0093

Division of Environmental Planning and Habitat Protection
Bureau of Wildlife Habitat Management
Pennsylvania Game Commission
2001 Elmerton Avenue
Harrisburg, PA 17110

Pennsylvania Department of Conservation and Natural Resources
Department of Conservation and Natural Resources
Rachel Carson State Office Building
PO Box 8767
400 Market Street
Harrisburg, PA 17105-8767

Pennsylvania Fish and Boat Commission
236 Lake Road
Somerset, PA 15501
Manor Township

Lancaster County Conservation District
1383 Arcadia Road, Room 200
Lancaster, PA 17601

Sprint Nextel
6391 Sprint Parkway
Overland Park, KS 66251-2650

www.ingramcontent.com/pod-product-compliance
Lightning Source LLC
Chambersburg PA
CBHW081235170526
45165CB00009B/3064